That Feels Earth!

Nature needs your help!

Our planet is getting warmer.

That means we will see less magical animals and plants.

It will be too hot for them!

But we can stop the earth heating up.
Then we can win back the wildlife!

These colourful creatures will show you how.

Helping feels earthmazing!

Look out for the lightbulbs for fun facts!

I'm refusing!

And that feels earthmazing!

Refusing toys and sweets helps tidy the planet.

 Refusing helps to save money.

 Refusing helps keep the air clean.

 Refusing saves on natural resources.

Take your time to think if you need something. It is okay to refuse a toy or sweet.

Reducing toys and sweets can tidy the planet.

 Reducing helps to save money.

 Reducing helps keep the air clean.

 Reducing saves on natural resources.

You can reduce by getting one packet of crisps instead of two!

I'm reusing.

An old shirt can be turned into a strong bag to carry things!

And that feels earthmazing!

Reusing turns handy resources into new things.

 Reusing means a cleaner outdoors.

 Reusing helps to save money.

 Reusing saves on natural resources.

You can reuse a baked bean can by turning it into a pencil pot.

I'm recycling!

And that feels earthmazing!

Recycling makes old things brand new again!

Recycling stops animals getting stuck.

Recycling helps keep the land nice and tidy.

Recycling saves on natural resources.

The council can tell you what resources can be recycled!

I'm moving.

By going outside and moving you will see more animals!

And that feels earthmazing!

You don't need a car to keep moving!

 Moving without a car keeps animals safe.

 Moving without a car keeps the air clean.

 Moving without a car makes you feel good!

You can move by walking or biking to school.

I'm saving water.

Water keeps us and the planet cool. It's important we save it!

And that feels earthmazing!

Saving water helps keep our rivers healthy.

 Saving water stops rivers going dry.

 Saving water helps to save money.

 Saving water saves on natural resources.

You can save water by having showers instead of baths!

Nature is the plants and animals around us!

 Helping nature makes animals grow strong.

 Helping nature helps keep the air clean.

 Helping nature makes plants grow.

Help nature by building a bug hotel. You can use straw, wood and fir cones!

I'm saving energy.

Energy uses lots of resources from the ground.

And that feels earthmazing!

Energy is what heats our homes.

 Saving energy helps to save money.

 Saving energy helps keep the air clean.

 Saving energy saves on natural resources.

Save energy by turning the heating down. You can put on a jumper to stay warm!

I'm saving power.

And that feels earthmazing!

Power keeps our lights on!

 Saving power helps to save money.

 Saving power helps keep the air clean.

 Saving power saves on natural resources.

You can save power by turning the lights off when you leave a room.

Growing your own food is planet and wildlife friendly!

 Growing food helps protect the land.

 Growing food helps keep the air clean.

 Growing food means less lorries.

You can make a yummy pie with fruit you have grown. Like some nice berries!

I'm feeding the animals!

Food gives animals lots of energy! That keeps them healthy.

And that feels earthmazing!

Feeding the animals helps them grow strong.

Feeding animals helps them feel good.

Feeding animals helps keep the land healthy.

Feeding animals helps plants grow.

You can feed the animals by putting out bird food.

I'm cleaning up.

And that feels earthmazing!

Cleaning up resources protects the land.

Cleaning up stops animals getting stuck.

Cleaning up keeps the land nice and tidy.

Cleaning up keeps water animals happy.

You can clean up by helping with beach cleans.

I'm playing with planet friendly toys.

And that feels earthmazing!

Planet friendly toys can be made at home!

 Planet friendly toys help protect the land.

 Planet friendly toys help keep the air clean.

 Planet friendly toys use less resources.

Home made play dough is a planet friendly fun toy!

You can talk to your friends to see if they can help.

 Talking to your friends helps you learn things.

 Talking to your friends helps you feel good.

 Talking to your friends makes them aware.

You can talk to your friends about helping the animals.

I'm doing my best
one day at a time.

And that also feels earthmazing!

The colourful creatures hope you enjoy their ideas!

Together we can help wildlife and the animals.

We can help the planet stay cool.

Let's bring back nature's magic!

It can be fun to help too.

It makes us feel good...

...and earthmazing!

Go to this website

thatsokay.co.uk

Find more resources online to help the planet!

© 2023 Chris Dixon. All rights reserved.

Printed and bound by CPI Group (UK) Ltd, Croydon, CR0 4YY
08/12/2023
03615774-0001